SKYFIXER

Gary V Anderson

Also by Gary V Anderson:

My Finnish Soul, 2010
Bunchgrass and Buttercups, 2012

Praise for SKYFIXER:

Moving to the rhythms of nature and the drum-beats of myths both personal and ancestral, Gary V Anderson's lyrical, many-tongued poems navigate the territory between mystery and clarity of vision. Incarnations of the poet—as logger, as soldier, as seeker—become layered upon each other toward the complexity of the whole. Places with names and specific points in time lead to regions without border, to insight and healing. A white horse or hermit thrush will signal the way. How fortunate we are to follow Anderson's restless, transcendent path, and further, to know "This journey's not over."

—John Willson, author of *Call This Room a Station*

What makes us pause at this place and moment? What do we take in, that holds us then urges us on? Grounded in a childlike wonder, most poetry avoids blunt declarations of intent. But in SKYFIXER, Gary V Anderson explains at the outset how a restless and damaged spirit scarred by war led him to search his physical and cultural roots, probing nature in a lifelong quest to locate and inhabit a deeper and more lasting home. This book follows the footsteps in his powerful healing journey—poems that triangulate meaning and insights beneath and beyond the confines of an ordinary life. In remote and isolated wanderings on this continent and in Finnish and Sámi lands, he watches and listens, and waits for the oddly familiar to come visiting. He often finds himself craving company, turning to us as if to a kindred spirit, saying "Wish you were here." And here he finds the wherewithal to ease the spirit, some healing in an old relationship with nature, beneath snow and rot finds a rusty tool meant to work well, still fitting the hand. It is a bracing journey worth the effort into what for many of us is a shared world we have dismissed at our peril, abused, taken advantage of, and thought long gone.

—Paul Hunter, author of *Sit a Tall Horse*.

As with most profound events and brushes with angels, it has taken time to assimilate and understand my fondness for this writer and his work. Where else in one's life can any of us look to find someone who has the courage to lean into the grief and trauma of their past and convey it into the welcoming arms of Mother Earth? Who knows someone who defies the space-time continuum in order to heal? Who else do we know that stands authentically as themselves, giving us permission to do so? Who among us understands that to heal, there is no better place to start than with the pain of our ancestors, and in doing so, connect ourselves to the work of humanity? When you read this work, do so with this in mind; Gary V Anderson is not just a writer, but a poet that turns tragedy into exquisite verse, he is a spiritual warrior, leading all of us who are brave enough to save our own lives.

—Tonia Stephanie Twigger, Seeker's Guide.

Seeking healing from trauma and loss, Gary V Anderson forges an intimate relationship with nature and the mythology of his ancestors. Anderson has listened deeply and connects intimately with his ancestors, himself and now with us.

—L.F. Hawk, (aka hsh) The Strongheart Clan

SKYFIXER

poetry

Cover Photo: Katherine Stickroth, Fishtrap
Outpost—2016, *Morning with Coyotes*

Author Photo: Roberta S. Lang

ISBN 978-0-578-65445-4

Printed in the United States of America
SHELTER BAY PUBLISHING
shelterbaypublishing.com
Portland, Oregon

For Roberta, who guides me through this healing and the hard forgiveness it demands.

Contents

Introduction

After being diagnosed with PTSD and anxiety related to my service in Viet Nam, I found a healer who read my poetry and described my writings as nature-based. Knowing that I was interested in learning more about my Sámi heritage, he suggested I explore my ancestors' indigenous spiritual practices as a way to begin healing from the war. This collection of poetry is a record of that exploration.

I have always found peace in nature, but on this healing path I have also found my voice, my heart and my soul. My search has taken me from connections locked in my DNA to soaring journeys with my spiritual guides. I have found the roots of my family in the far north of Scandinavia and a deeper appreciation of those closer to home.

I am fond of saying that I am filling my soul with places—places that have their own language and spirits. I was raised in rural Southwest Washington and have added the Upper Peninsula of Michigan, Finland, Norway and Sweden to my nature.

It's important for me to share these poems with family and friends, those I know and those I've yet to meet. With that in mind, a number of poems in this collection have been translated into Northern Sámi, Finnish, Swedish, and Norwegian.

I embrace the translations and consider them a collaboration and enhancement of the art of poetry. The collaboration may produce alternate meanings and nuance which I welcome. I, alone, take responsibility for any differences in description and meaning—I consider all as synchronicity.

Men think they are better than grass…

from "The River of Bees"
W. S. Merwin 1993

I

Nature-based Poems
That Changed My Life

From *Bunchgrass and Buttercups,* 2012:

Deep River Finn
Onkalo
Dividing the Farm

From *My Finnish Soul,* 2010:

You Took a Wrong Turn
Forester's Prayer
Eulogy

Deep River Finn

Nature is solitude,
not meant for entertainment.
You stay home, friend,

leave me to my longing.

At sunrise
in the Willapa Hills,
the robin begins,
solo, A cappella.

Onkalo

Finnish for hiding place

Return to a place
once lived,
find something
once lost.

Hold undamaged
parts of soul and self
as dew settles
on lowlands.

Find the cedar stump
burned hollow,
pull the sword fern
door closed,
dig for childish artifacts
buried there.

Touch flat rocks
from fast water,
say *skyfixer*,
say *dreamstream*.

Cry,
finally cry,
for the boy.

Dividing the Farm

You take fences,
tilled fields,
straight lines,
square corners
of forty.
Give me
meander of
stream, bank of
cattails, willow.

You take tree farm,
clear cut.
Give me
tangle of swamp,
knoll above marsh where
salt meets fresh,
vernal pond where
salamanders arrive
one spring night from
down under woody debris.

You took a wrong turn

at the sugar bush,
its rusted sap buckets and copper boiler
scattered on the forest floor.

If you had waded Katy Creek
and walked up the rutted skid trail,
you would have found the
old growth basswood, maple
and yellow birch.

You might have found the
secret room in the sandstone grotto
with its fern-covered walls
and floor of leaves.

Instead, you took the trail to
the crescent of the beaver dam,
around the vernal pond and
into the lost canyon.

I wondered if you heard
the black-throated blue, the mourning warbler
or the hermit thrush in the
dense, damp, lush of the stream bottom.

I wondered if you found a place
where ashes could begin their journey
down those spring-fed brooks,
to Deer Lake, through Superior, to the sea.

Forester's Prayer

The trees are my cathedral,
spring-fed brooks my baptismal,
snowshoes my life raft.

Silence my meditation,
blue jays my sentinel,
budding maples the promise.

The spirit guide, my compass,
helps me go where I ought to go,
do as I ought to do.

Eulogy

For Marie, the best damned fisherwoman a dozer
operator could have hoped to know.

Those were the last best days.

Diesel smoke and mineral soil,
the good earth smells of logging
on the upper Naselle.

Down stream,
the uneven ground of the riverbank
welcomed the fresh-caught steelhead,
an oki-drifter hanging from its mouth.

One more cast before the cat skinner comes home.

Another

Another

II

Healers

33. I beat these images
on the stone, on the drum

it is so slow

after drumming for a while
I am pulled into another world

to visions

Nils-Aslak Valkeapää, BEAIVI, ÁHČÁŽAN, THE
SUN, MY FATHER.

House of the Longest Night

They were raptor, shape-shifted, merged, soaring
over the vernal pond in the valley of the lost canyon,
searching for the cave they both knew was there.

Wings folded to their side, they dove through portal
dark, to the bottom, into glowing light, caught a
thermal above a stone floor and a ring of white horses.

One earth

one heart,

drumbeat,

same beat,

healing,

in the house of the

longest night.

There was high ground above the pond and the entrance to the canyon. Skookum appeared where the stream entered the pond as spring runoff.

Together, they walked into the canyon. Skookum asked him to find a smooth rock and blow fear into it. They buried the rock among the roots of a large pine and sat by that tree for a time; he and Skookum, his ally.

Let blue

reindeer eyes

move to gold,

solstice to solstice,

winter to summer.

Out of darkness

into light.

He asked Skookum to meet at the vernal pond. As he walked through the meadow to greet Skookum, he looked back over his shoulder.

They sat under the pine and a light came down through the branches, through them into the earth. They smiled at one another and Skookum asked, "Why do you look back?"

The hinge,

a pivot,

on swinging gate

or door.

Forth and back,

memories released

in passing,

one room,

one meadow,

to the next.

Skookum led him to the sacred tree, climbed with him and pushed him past the reaches of the pine, into the upper world. When he arrived, he was greeted by a Sámi noaidi and invited into a lavvu to sit by the fire.

The drum appeared, adorned with lines and symbols drawn on the skin. Noaidi instructed him to fashion a map of his journeys and share the ancient knowledge.

Leave this earthly place,

lock on a vector,

expect no end.

Fly over northern lights,

dance on the horizon.

Hang ribbons,

drop crumbs,

blaze trees—return,

upon distant drumbeats.

What We Know

My logger friend
paused on our snowshoe walk
and said,
something happened here.

He scraped through
early snow,
then moss,
with his boot;
revealed broken crosscut saw,
runners from sled,
forgotten tools of long ago.

We sat talking
about the war,
difficult work of healing,
loss of soul.
He scraped snow
from my shoulder,
and said,
something happened here.

We talked of our struggles and I recalled a
journey:

A healer appeared with an
opening in his heart.
Orange light and eyes of a
raptor were visible. The healer placed a
ring of orange on my body and a
raptor came out of my heart.
He said, your ancestors acknowledged
your knowing, your seeing.

My friend asked,
maybe you could find the
ax I lost here last summer?

Murmuration

I tasted fear when you
pushed your kayak
into the water at
Point No Point.
Did you not see the
murmuration of Dunlin?
Did you not feel
wings beating continuous
protection in mass?
Did you not know
trauma is a life sentence?
And what about the
voices saying,
don't go it alone?

Voices of Oulanka

We stopped in the forest,
by the river, for coffee.
Hands folded in his lap,
he said in a hushed voice,
mummo could see illness and
impending death. She was a healer.
The ill were taken to her
instead of a doctor.
She disguised her powers by using a
tourniquet and forest herbs
when healing,
so as not to be called a witch.

I came for this.
Filling my soul with places,
coffee ceremonies in the forest,
stories that began with mummo,
knowing, seeing.
Old men staring into fire,
recalling advice, cautions,
bringing all to nature for healing.

Mummo said, *"When you
go to the forest with
papa, you must be silent if you
want to see the foxes."*

And I remember, *"Grandpa,
when we walk in the forest,
I hear voices."*

III

Return of the Light

Skyfixer Journal

It's whisper time.
After daylight,
before sunrise.
You meditate in silence,
listen for gaps in
sound and thought.

From this perch, above
Camp Creek Canyon, you imagine
Chief Joseph's horses, women in blankets.
Your eyes move along their route and you
realize you are not the first to cry here.

Your drum speaks of
   images within images,
   journeys within journeys,
   metaphor within metaphor;
   masks of ancient secrets.

Raise your Sámi yoik,
to the spirits
   of prairie,
   of sunrise,
   of guides and helpers,
   of earth.

Water, look what you have
done. Welcome the seep.
Absorb artifacts of
layered landscapes,
convergence of chronology.

Not all answers yet evident.
Some found in a portal,
in a canyon,
just over the horizon.

As the last echoes of
drumbeats
rumble to the prairie,
your knees weaken,
breath labors.

This journey's not over.

Bright green sound moves
through your head;
music heard and seen.

Not scales of your
A-minor childhood;
no longing in these
hopeful chords.

Then—birdsong:

> Western Meadowlark
> Vesper Sparrow

Out of the Shadows

A ceremony was held for an aging soldier. After five decades, a veteran was awarded a medal for wounds suffered to his soul.

Voices could be heard from a far-off lake in Sápmi. Young retrieved soul parts,—silly, playful, and talkative—came to join the ceremony. They were happy to be back. There was much joy and celebration.

The soldier was escorted from the parade grounds by a lone white horse.

When does a soldier
lose parts of soul?
What moment marks
the silent departure?
When fear is gained?
Or when fear is lost?
Flee, wait,
hide among animals
and healing spirits,
survive.

IV

Postcards from the Forest

Postcard 122 A.D.

I am out here on
Hadrian's wall. I
suppose you were
expecting one of those
Vindolanda postcards. But
Octavius cut all the
birch, alder and oak.
Nothing left to fashion the
diptychs and could find no
gum Arabic for ink.

Wish you were here.

I am Nature

He found the bed of the moose and her calf.
They slept here last night;
flattened grass, one large, one small.
Steps from his cabin,
as to honor and protect.
They know his name.

At sunrise,
after the drum,
after the yoik,
they drifted into aspen and pine.

He lay face down in their beds chanting:
I am nature, I AM nature, I am NATURE.

No dominion,
no over,
in these words.

Wish you were here.

All About Bracken

Bracken.
Vascular,
ubiquitous,
rhizome.
Gently tugging
ankles,
beckoning,
joining the lush of
forest grass and
banana slugs.

The senses remain,
only the signals have
changed—or maybe the
reverse.
I am the boy in
grass, under bracken,
crawling to sunlight,
making spears.

Wish you were here.

Edge of the Earth

Slept in true light.
No ambient here on
shore of Lake Superior. This
morning of mosquitoes, then
warblers—black-throated blue,
yellow-rumped. No
song equal to
hermit thrush last
night.

Then northern lights.

Wish you were here.

Do the Math

There are six words for love in Greek
and six words for gender in Hebrew.

Consider the possibilities.

Wish you were here.

Beyond the Tent

When the green meets the
gold—sunset in the prairie.
Wake up the coyotes,
make preparations for the kill,
savor sweet deer, perhaps elk.

No rodents for us tonight.

Wish you were here.

Govadas

The drum,

a thing
out of which
pictures come.
Ride the hoof beats
out of the solar
system to distant
worlds. Follow
ancestors to
secret knowledge.

Wish you were here.

Colonization

Frontiers and fences—
a romantic notion.

One man's frontier,
another's indigenous home.

And fences—
well, they beget
yours and mine.

Just sayin'.

Wish you were here.

Self-Portrait

In old growth, see
towering hemlocks.
Look to forest floor,
find smaller in
shade of giants,
identical age, waiting
for big guys to
fall.

Wish you were here.

Istua

Finnish for sit

She pats the
dusty porch step,
says, *istua.*

Neither of us
know the
importance of
clean steps to
signal the
condition
inside this
Finnish home.

Wish you were here.

Keep the Fire Burning

Mindful of the
ancient master sauce,
she added a
pinch of this, a
glass of that,
respecting grandma's
book of secret recipes.

Wish you were here.

Rough-Sawn Wood

A pair of barn swallows
found their way to
eaves of the converted
logging shack;
separated from our bed by
layers of ship lap
and cedar shingles,
adding their notes to the
drumbeat of spring.

Water-stains on
ceiling boards,
made lion, horse,
and moon.
We reached to
touch rough edges,
wondered about
Grandpa's saw.

Wish you were here.

Other People's Words

"...the shadows...saw nothing but a young girl on her
honeymoon. And she knew...the fire would start to
fade. She thought of heat. She thought of time."
Bill Morrissey, "Birches", Night Train, 1993.

The poems were coming
regular as newlywed
wood. Was it birch or oak?

Burning bright or long—
a flash, or glowing embers?

In those days
only *Tom Robbins* was
known to make love stay.

Wish you were here.

Breivik Norway

Full moon Finnmark night,

Sámi Sállen now Sørøya,

Nine thousand reindeer.

Wish you were here.

Lament

I know rivers.

Yellow Dog,
Fox,
Laughing Whitefish.

Helped save Big Two—Hearted,
but could not save the
beech trees.

Wish you were here.

V

Fragments

Ruoantähteet

Finnish for leftovers, scraps

If I were to write another poem,
I would talk about substitutes—
golf courses for savannahs,
sport for war,
stem cells to repair broken hearts.

I would paint over tough times,
but not that rough-water trip to
Rocky Point, with Grandpa,
salvaging lumber,
chasing seagulls.

The least you need to know as I age—
don't talk about me in past tense,
don't bring up the solace of winter solstice,
or the idea that testes and ovaries
shrink with lower temperatures
and are digested in birds
as they migrate.
That kind of talk
makes me twitchy.

I'm looking forward to
the risotto trinity,
where I follow my mink trail,
where all bad things are
imagined away—
where I remember a Sunday morning,
see my old man downhill,
next to the outhouse—
after a direct hit
from a well-aimed alder block—
Sears catalog in one hand,
Daily Astorian in the other,
logger pants at his ankles,
screaming like Charles Bukowski.

I have rituals to prepare
for what comes next—
get ready for the real work,
think longer,
say less,
pour a dram of single malt,
meditate.

Journal Entry # 354—
His Name Was #4 Boy

…he could hear the drum and found himself in a stone room with a large elephant. Then he was on the back of the elephant and rode there for a time. Soon, the large elephant turned into a small elephant, a stuffed toy under his arm. He walked a gravel road to his old home place in Deep River. His mom and dad were there on the porch looking at him, smiling and talking in a very animated way. The scene was in brown tones as in an old Kodachrome movie. He could not hear what they were saying, but they were arm in arm and he was surprised by a feeling they were in love with each other and talking about him as if they were proud and approving.

Journal Entry # 582—Learning How to Heal

…he was made to lie down on the ground. He left his body and was watching from above. He could see his skeleton and bones as the assembled Shamans removed pieces of his flesh. A blanket was placed over him. He was lifted to stand. As he began to walk away from the Shamans, the blanket changed to a flowing robe. He felt as if he was being cleansed and prepared for some event or major change.

Advice from Lapland

For Jukka, Rauno and Mika

When lost in the forest—
build a fire,
boil coffee,
cook sausages
if you have them.
Go home.

VI

Northern Sámi Translations
Almmi quvhllár—Northern
Sámi for Skyfixer

Translated to Northern Sámi by:

Ritva Torikka of Inari, Finland

Ritva has been a journalist at Yle Sápmi for
30 years. She has been working as a reporter
in news and current affairs and as producer
in children-tv in Sámi. She has also worked
with translations into Northern Sámi, as in
Tove Jansson's "Moominpappa at Sea" book
and as a main translator artist for Outi Pieski's
and researcher Eeva-Kristiina Harlin's book
"Rematriation of the Foremother's Crown."

Deep River suopmelaš

Luondu lea ieš,
ii oaivvilduvvon hearvan.
Biso ruovttus, ustiban,

divtte mu áibbašit.

Iđitguksos
Willaba dieváid alde,
guovssoloddi lávlugoahtá,
a cappella.

Onkalo

suomagillii čiehkádanbáiki, hoallu

Máhca dohko,
gos oktii orro
gávnna juoga,
man oktii láhppe.

Doala gitta sielu rihkkašuvakeahtes osiin
ja iešvuođas,
go suoldni
luoitáda vuolleeatnamiidda.

Gávnna boldojuvvon hoallu
sedermuora guddos,
hilske gáiskkiid
gittauvssaid,
rokka dohko čihkkojuvvon
mánnávuođa diŋggaid.

Njávkkat bávttiid, maid
golgi čázit leat dulben
daja *almmi guvhllár*
daja *nieguid rávdnji.*

Čiero,
čiero viimmatge,
bártni dihtii.

Eanadálu juogadeapmi

Váldde don áiddiid,
plovejuvvon bealdduid,
njuolggo linnjáid,
čiegaid,
njealljelogi njealjahasmehtera.
Atte munnje
joga mohki, gáddedearpmi
dan šattuiguin, sieđgga.

Váldde don vuovddi,
báljisin čuhppojuvvon.
Atte munnje
jekkiid dukki
Buncci jeaggeeatnama bajábealde,
doppe gos sáltečáhci deaivvada sáivačáziin,
giđđaláddo, gosa salamanderat bohtet
giđđat ovtta ija
smáhkuid vuolde.

Jorggihit boastut

sohkarmiestagiid siste,
ruston máihlelihtit ja veaikespánjat
miehtá.

Jos ledjet gállit Katy Creek -ádjagis
ja vázzi gollan čierastanluotta bajás,
ledjet gávdnat boares ninnamuora, váhtára ja
fiskes soagi.

Ledjet maid gávdnat
sáttogeađgehoallu suollemas lanja
man seinniin gáiskkit
ja láhttis lasttat

Muhto don mannet bálgá mielde
mádjit buođu jorbálasa guvlui
giđđaláddo birra
láhppon ávžái.

Smiehtan, gulletgo
čáhppesčotta vizara
dahje oktoorut rástá
deahtta, lákta, šattolaš jogabotnis.

Smiehtan, gávdnetgo báikki,
gos gunat sáhtašedje álggahit mátkkiset
vulos gáldoádjagiid mielde,
Deer Lake-jávrái, Superiora čađa ja de merrii.

Vuovdebargi rohkos

Muorat leat mu girku,
gáldoádjagat mu gásttašeapmi,
muohtagápmagat mu gádjunláhttá

Jaskatvuohta mu meditašuvdna
alitdiehppelátteguovssat mu fákta,
váhtára álggut lohpádus.

Vuoigŋaofelaš, mu kompassa,
veahkeha mu deaivat dohko gosa galggan,
dahkat dan maid galggan.

Muitosáhka

Mariei, buoremus fántena guolásteaddjinissonii,
gean tráktorvuoddji sáhtii alcces sávvat.

Dat ledje maŋimuš buoremus beaivvit.

Sulára suovva ja minerálaeana,
buori eatnamis lea vuovdečuohppama hádja
bajit Naselles.

Vuollin
johkadearpmi borit
sávve buresboahtima easkka goddon dápmohii,
mas okivuogga heaŋgái njálbmečiegas

Oktii vel šlivge mášenvuoddji ovdalgo boahtá
ruoktot

Vel oktii

Oktii vel

Guhkimus ija viessu

Soai leigga gazzalottit, molson hámi, oktii suddan,
sattáhalaiga giđđaláddo bajábealde láhppon ávžži
leagis, ozaiga doppe hoallu, man guktot diđiiga doppe
leat.

Soaját siidduid vuostá, soai buokčaleigga uksaráiggi
seavdnjadasa čađa, gitta bodnái, šerres čuvgii, fáhtiiga
lieggasa geađgás eatnama ja vilges heasttaid rieggá
bajábealde.

Okta eana

okta váibmu.

Rumbbu jietna

seamma coahkkin

buorideaddji,

guhkimus ija

viesus.

Ávženjálmmis láddo bajábealde lei dievvá. Skookum iđii dakko gokko čáhci luittii ádjaga mielde láddui.

Ovtta fáro soai vácciiga ávžái. Skookum dáhtui su ohcat jorbá geađggi ja bossut balu dan sisa. Soai hávdádeigga geađggi stuorra beazi ruohttasiid gaskii ja čohkohalaiga dan máddagis oanehaš; son ja Skookum, su verdde.

Divtte alit

bohccočalmmiid

šaddat gollin,

áigejorggáldaga áigejorggáldahkan,

dálvvi geassin.

Seavdnjadasas

čuvgii.

Son dáhtui Skookuma deaivvadit suinna giđđaláddo luhtte. Go váccii niittu čađa buorástahttit Skookuma, son geahčai oalggis badjel maŋosguvlui.

Soai čohkkáiga beahcemáddagis ja čuovga báittii ovssiid čađa, sudno čađa eatnama sisa. Soai mojohalaiga goappat guoibmáseaskka ja Skookum jearai, "Manin don geahčat maŋos?"

Sárán,

dego lađas,

sugadeaddji verráhis

dahje uvssas.

Ovddos maŋos,

muittuid luvven

nuo fal,

okta latnja,

okta niitu,

ja de čuovvovaš.

*Skookum doalvvui su bassi muora lusa, gavccui suinna
ja duvdilii su beahcegierragiid bajábeallái, bajit
máilbmái. Go son ollii, Sámi Noaidi dearvvahii su ja
bovdii lávvui dollagáddái.*

*Meavrresgárri iđii, govvosiiguin ja mearkkaiguin
hervejuvvon. Noaidi rávvii su hábmet mátkkiinis gárttá
ja juogadit dološ dieđu.*

Vuolgge dán eatnanlaš báikkis,

mearret mátkki meari,

ale vuordde geaži.

Girdde guovssahasaid badjel,

dánsso almmiravddas.

Heaŋggo báttiid,

goaikkut moaluid,

buollat muoraid—máhca,

ovttafáro rumbbu jienain,

mii gullo guhkkelis.

Oulanka jienat

Moai bisáneimme vuovddis,
johgáttis, gáfestallat.
Gieđat askái máhccojuvvon,
son dajai fiinna jienain,
mummo nagodii oaidnit buohcuvuođa
ja jápmima, mii lea lahka. Son lei guvhllár.
Buohcciid dolvo su lusa, eai doaktára lusa.
Son čiegai fámuidis
go guvhllárasttii,
čanastagaiguin ja šattuiguin
amas noaidin gohčoduvvot.

Bohten dán dihtii.
Deavdit sielu báikkiiguin,
gáfestallanvieruiguin vuovddis,
Muitalusaiguin, mat álget mummos,
su dieđuin, oaidnimis.
Boares albmát stirrájit dollii,
vurdet dieđu, ráđi,
máhcahit buot lundui buorránit.

Mummo dajai,
"Go manat meahccái ádjáin
don galggat leat jaska
jos háliidat oaidnit riebaniid."

Ja muittán, *"Áddjá,*
go moai vázze meahcis,
gulan jienaid."

Almmiguvhllára beaivegirji

Savkkástallama áigi.
Beaivečuovgga maŋŋá,
ovdal beaivváža badjáneami.
Smiehtadalat jaskatvuođas,
guldalat bottuid
jienain ja jurdagiin.

Dán holgga alde,
Camp Creek ávžži bajábealde,
imaštalat hoavda Josepha heasttaid,
nissoniid ránuineaset.
Du čalmmit čuvodit sin johtinbálgáid
ja áddet, don it leat vuosttas, gii čierru dáppe.

Du rumbu hállá
    govain govaid siste,
    mátkkiin mátkkiid siste,
    veardádusain veardádusaid siste
    dološ suollemasvuođaid maskeradain.

Rohtte iežat luođi
    preria,
    eahketroađi,
    ofelaččaid ja vehkiid,
    eatnama
    vuoiŋŋaide.

Čáhci, geahča maid leat
dahkan. Sáva buresboahtima vuohččumii.
Njama alccet gerdojuvvon duovdagiid
buktagiid,
áigelogu lahkoneami.

Eai buot vástádusat leat vel oidnosis.
Muhtimat gávdnon uvssohis,
ávžžis,
aiddo fal almmiravdda bajábealde.

Go rumbbu časkkástaga
maŋimuš skájat
juraidit preriai,
du čippit hedjonit,
vuoiŋŋanasat lossot.
Dát mátki ii leat meattá.

Šerres ruoná jietna johtá
du oaivvi čađa;
musihkka, mii gullo ja oidno.

Eai du a-molla mánnávuođa
ceahkkálasat;
ii áibbašeapmi
dáid vuordevaš akordain.

Ja de—cizáža lávlun:

    Vizardeaddji prerialeivvoš
    Amerihká niitocihci

Eret suoivaniid siste

Boares soalddáhii dollojuvvui seremoniija. Bealle jahkečuođi
maŋŋá, veterána bálkkašuvvui medáljain daid háviid
ovddas, main su siellu lei gillán.

Guhkkin Sámi jávrri alde sáhtii gullat jienaid.
Máhcahuvvon nuorra bihtát sielus,—hearvás, skálžžáris ja
hállái—bohte searvat seremoniijai. Dat ledje lihkolaččat go
ledje máhccan. Dat buvttii olu ilu ja ávvudeami.

Oktonas vilges heasta mieđuštii soalddáha parádašiljus eret.

Goas soalddát massá
osiid sielustis?
Makkár mearka lea dan
jaskes vuolgima bottus?
Goas fáhtehallá ballui?
Dahje goas ballu lea jávkan?
Báhtar, vuordde,
čiehkádala ealliid ja dálkkodeaddji vuoiŋŋaid gaskkas,
ceavzze.

VII

Finnish Translations
Taivaankorjaaja—Finnish for Skyfixer

Translated to Finnish by:

Sonia Luokkala, Homer, Alaska

Born and raised in Finland, Sonia has worked as an investigative reporter and photojournalist on environmental and indigenous issues for over a decade and is currently transitioning to film. She moved to the States in 2012, and lives in coastal Alaska, where she continues to foster Finnish ancestral traditions.

Suomessa syntynyt ja kasvanut Sonia on työskennellyt journalistina ja kuvajournalistina yli vuosikymmenen. Hän muutti Yhdysvaltoihin vuonna 2012 ja asuu Alaskassa, missä hän jatkaa suomalaisten kansanperinteiden harjoittamista.

Suomalainen Deep Riveristä

Luonto on yksineloa,
ei tarkoitettu viihteeksi.
Pysy kotona, ystävä,

jätä minut kaihoni pariin.

Auringon noustessa
Willapan vuoristossa,
punarinta aloittaa soolon,
A cappella.

Onkalo

Palaa paikkaan
ennen asuttuun,
löydä jotakin
kerran kadotettua.

Pitele haavoittumattomia
sielun ja itsen osia
kasteen asetuttua
alangoille.

Löydä seetripuun kanto
palanut onkalo,
kitke saniainen
suljetuin ovin,
kaiva esiin sinne haudattuja
lapsenomaisia esineitä.

Kosketa nopeasti virtaavien vesien
tasoittamia kallioita
sano *taivaakorjaaja,*
sano *unenvirta.*

Itke,
vihdoin itke,
pojan vuoksi.

Tilan jakaminen

Ota aidat,
viljellyt pellot,
suorat viivat,
neliönmuotoisia nurkkia
neljäkymmentä.
Anna minulle
virran mutka,
käämäsärkkä, paju.

Ota talousmetsä,
avohakattu.
Anna minulle
suon vyyhti,
kumpare suomaan yltä missä
suola tapaa makean,
kevätlammen minne
salamanterit saapuvat
eräänä kevätyönä
puukatteen alta.

Käännyit väärin

Sokerivaahterametsä,
ruosteiset mahlaämpärit ja kuparikattila
maastossa hajallaan.

Jos olisit kahlannut Katy Creekissä,
ja kävellyt yli uratun liukureitin,
olisit löytänyt
aarniolehmuksen, vaahteran
ja keltakoivun.

Olisit saattanut löytää
hiekkakiviluolan salaisen huoneen
saniaisten peittämine seinineen
ja pohjan lehtikerroksen.

Sen sijaan, otit polun
kohti majavan padon puolikuuta,
kevätlammen ympäri ja
kadotettuun kanjoniin.

Mietin, jos kuulit sinikerttulin, korpikerttulin
tai erakkorastaan
tiheän, kostean, rehevän virran pohjassa.

Mietin, jos löysit paikan
mistä tuhkat aloittaisivat matkansa
lähteen ruokkimia puroja pitkin,
Deer Lake-järveen, Yläjärveen, mereen.

Metsänhoitajan Rukous

Puut ovat katedraalini,
lähteenruokkimat purot kasteeni,
lumikengät pelastuslauttani.

Hiljaisuus meditaationi,
sinitöyhtönärhet vartijani,
orastavat vaahterat, lupaus.

Henkiopas, kompassini,
auttaa kulkemaan minne tulee kulkea,
tekemään mitä tulee tehdä.

Muistopuhe

Marielle, parhaalle kalastajanaiselle mitä
puskutraktorin
ajaja olisi koskaan voinut pyytää.

Ne olivat päivistä parhaita.

Dieselin savua ja kivennäismaata,
hyvä maa tuoksuu hakkuilta
ylemmässä Nasellessa.

Alavirralla,
joentörmän kumpuileva maasto
vastaanotti juuri pyydetyn taimenen,

oki-syötti suussaan.
Vielä yksi ongenheitto ennen kuin kaivurikuski
saapuu kotiin.

Yksi vielä

Yksi vielä

Pisimmän Yön Talo

He olivat petolintuja, muotonsa muuttaneita, yhteen sulautuneita, liitäen kevätlampien yllä kadonneen kanjonin laaksossa, etsiessään luolaa, jonka nmolemmat tiesivät olevan siellä.

Siipensä kylkiinsä taittaen, he sukelsivat halki pimeän portaalin, pohjaan saakka, hehkuvaan valoon, loysivät termiikin kivisen maaston ja valkoisten hevosten kehän yllä.

Yksi maa

yksi sydän,

rummunlyönti,

sama tahti,

parantava,

pisimmän yön

talossa.

Lammen yllä ja kanjonin sisäänkäynnissä oli kohouma. Skookum ilmaantui sinne, missä vesi virtasi lampeen puron valumana.

Yhdessä, he kävelivät kanjoniin. Skookum pyysi häntä etsimään sileän kiven ja puhaltamaan pelon sen sisään. He hautasivat kiven suuren männyn juurikkoon ja istuivat puun vieressä hetken; hän ja Skookum, liittolaisensa.

Anna sinisten

poronsilmien

muuttua kullaksi,

tasauksesta tasaukseen,

talvesta kesään.

Ulos pimeydestä

valoon.

Hän pyysi Skookumia tapaamaan kevätlammella.
Kävellessään niityn halki tervehtimään Skookumia,
hän katsoi olkansa yli taakseen.

He istuivat männyn juurella ja valo laskeutui oksien
lävitse, heidän lävitseen, maan sisään. He hymyilivät
toisilleen ja Skookum kysyi, "Miksi katsot takaisin?"

Se sarana,

keskipiste,

keinuvassa portissa

tai ovessa.

Edestakaisin,

muistoja vapautui

ohimennen,

yksi huone,

yksi niitty,

seuraava.

Skookum johdatti hänet pyhän puun luokse, kiipesi
hänen kanssaan ja työnsi hänet männyn korkeuksien
ulottumattomiin, yliseen. Kun hän saapui, häntä
tervehti noaidi ja hänet kutsuttiin laavuun tulen äärelle
istumaan.

Ilmaantui nahkaan piirretyin viivoin ja symbolein
koristettu noitarumpu. Noiaidi ohjasi häntä
muotoilemaan matkoistaan kartan ja jakamaan
ikiaikaisen tiedon.

Jätä tämä maallinen paikka,

aseta kurssisi,

odota sen jatkuvan.

Lennä ylitse revontulten,

tanssi horisontissa.

ripusta nauhoja,

pudota murusia,

sytytä puita—palaa,

kaukaisten rummunlyöntien yllä.

Oulangan Äänet

Pysähdyimme metsään,
joen ääreen, kahvittelemaan.
Kädet syliinsä taitettuna,
hän sanoi hiljaisella äänellä,
Mummo kykeni näkemään sairauden ja
lähenevän kuoleman. Hän oli parantaja.
Lääkärin sijaan
sairaat tuotiin hänen luokseen.
Hän salasi kykynsä
parantaessaan puristussiteillä ja metsän yrteillä,
jotta ei olisi kutsuttu noidaksi.

Tämän vuoksi tulin tänne.
Täyttääkseni sieluni paikoilla,
kahviseremonioilla metsässä,
kertomuksilla jotka alkoivat mummosta,
tietämisestä, näkemisestä.
Tuleen katsoen, vanhat miehet
palauttavat mieliinsä neuvoja, varoituksia,
tuovat kaiken luontoon eheytymään.

Mummo sanoi, *"Kun*
menet metsään papan kanssa
sinun täytyy olla hiljaa jos
tahdot nähdä ketut.

Ja muistan, *"Pappa,*
kun kävelemme metsässä,
kuulen ääniä."

Taivaankorjaajan Päiväkirja

On kuiskausten aika.
Päivänvalon jälkeen,
ennen auringonlaskua.
Meditoit hiljaisuudessa,
kuuntelet taukoja
äänessä ja ajatuksessa.

Tältä orrelta,
Camp Creek kanjonin yllä, kuvittelet
intiaanipäällikkö Josephin hevoset, naiset
vilteissään.
Silmäsi seuraavat heidän reittiään ja
huomaat, et ole ensimmäinen joka on itkenyt
täällä.

Rumpusi kertoo
    kuvista kuvien sisällä,
    matkoista matkojen sisällä,
    metaforista metaforien sisällä;
    ikiaikaisten salaisuuksien naamioita.

Kohota joikusi
preerian,
auringonnousun,
opasten ja auttajien,
maan
hengille.

Vesi, katso mitä olet
tehnyt. Vastaanota vuoto.
Omaksu kerroksittaisten maisemien
artifaktit,
ajanlaskun lähentyminen.

Kaikki vastaukset eivät ole vielä selkeitä.
Jotkut löytyvät portaalista,
kanjonista,
aivan horisontin yltä.

Rummunlyöntien
viimeisten kaikujen
jylähtäessä preerialle,
polvesi heikentyvät,
hengitys vaikeutuu.

Tämä matka ei ole ohi.

Kirkkaanvihreä ääni liikkuu
pääsi läpi;
nähty ja kuultu
musiikki.

Eivät A-molli lapsuutesi
asteikkoja;
ei kaipausta näissä
toiveikkaissa soinnuissa.

Sitten—linnunlaulu:

Huilupreeriaturpiaali
Amerikanniittysirkku

Varjoista Ulos

*Ikääntyvälle sotilaalle pidettiin seremonia. Viiden
vuosikymmenen jälkeen veteraanille annettiin mitali
sielunsa kärsimistä haavoista.
Saamenmaan kaukaiselta järveltä kuului ääniä.
Palautetut nuoret sielun palaset,—hauskat, leikkisät
ja puheliaat—saapuivat ottamaan osaa seremoniaan.
He olivat onnellisia siitä, että olivat palanneet. Seurasi
paljon iloa ja juhlintaa.*

*Yksinäinen valkoinen hevonen saattoi sotilaan
paraatikentältä.*

Milloin sotilas
menettää sielunsa osia?
Mikä hetki merkitsee
sen hiljaisen lähdön?

Milloin on pelko omaksuttu?
Tai milloin on pelko hävitetty?
Pakene, odota,
piileksi eläinten ja parantavien henkien luona,
selviydy.

VIII

Swedish Translations

Translated to Swedish by:

Linnea Lindblom, Inverness, Skottland.

Deep River Finn	Djupa Finnfloden
Onkalo	Onkalo
Dividing the Farm	Uppdelning av gården
You Took a Wrong Turn	Du tog fel väg
Forester's Prayer	Skogsarbetarens bön
Eulogy	Eloge
House of the Longest Night	Huset av den längsta natten
Voices of Oulanka	Oulankas röster
Skyfixer Journal	Skyfixers dagbok
Out of the Shadows	Ute ur skuggorna

Djupa Finnfloden

Naturen är ensamhet,
inte menat för underhållning.
Stanna du hemma, vän,

lämna mig till min längtan.

Vid soluppgången
i Willapa Hills,
börjar rödhaken,
solitär, instrumentlös.

Onkalo

Finska för gömställe

Återvänd till en plats,
en gång levd på,
hitta någonting
en gång förlorat.

Håll oskadade
delar av själ och själv
när dagg stillnar
på lågländerna.

Hitta cedarstubben
bränd ihålig,
stäng igen dörren av
svärdbräken,
gräv efter barnsliga artefakter
begravna där.

Rör vid flata stenar
från rusande vatten,
säg *skyfixer*,
säg *dreamstream*.

Gråt,
gråt äntligen,
för pojken.

Uppdelning av gården

Du tar stängsel,
brukade fält,
raka linjer,
fyrkantiga hörn
på fyrtio.
Ge mig
meanderslingor, sandbanken
med kaveldun, vide.

Du tar skogsodling,
kalhugget.
Ge mig,
hoptrasslade träsk,
kullen ovanför kärret där
salt möter färskt,
vårdammar där
salamandrar anländer
en vårnatt från
undersidan av träbråte.

Du tog fel väg

vid sockerskogen,
dess rostiga savhinkar och kopparkittel
utspridda på skogsbotten.

Om du hade vadat Katy Creek,
och vandrat upp det fårade lunnarspåret,
hade du hittat urskogen av svartlind,
lönn och gulbjörk.

Du kanske hade hittat det
hemliga rummet i sandstensgrottan
med sina ormbunkstäckta väggar
och golv av löv.

Istället tog du stigen till
bäverdammens kurva,
runt vårdammen och
in i den förlorade kanjonen.

Jag undrade om du hörde
den blåryggade skogssångaren,
sorgskogssångaren,
eller eremitskogstrasten i den
täta, fuktiga, lummigheten på strömbotten.

Jag undrar om du hittade en plats
där askar kunde börja sin resa
ner de där vårfyllda bäckarna,
till Deer Lake, genom Superior, till havet.

Skogsarbetarens bön

Träden är min katedral,
vårfyllda bäckar mitt dop,
snöskor min räddningsflotte.

Tystnad min meditation,
blåskrikor min vaktpost,
knoppande lönnar mitt löfte.

Andeguiden, min kompass,
hjälper mig att gå dit jag borde gå,
göra som jag borde göra.

Eloge

Åt Marie, den bästa fiskarkvinna
en schaktförare kunde ha hoppats på att känna.

Det var de sista bästa dagarna.

Dieselrök och mineraljord,
de goda jorddofterna av skogsavverkning
vid övre Naselle.

Nedströms,
den ojämna marken av flodbanken
välkomnade den nyfångade regnbågsöringen,
ett oki-driftflöte hängande från dess mun.

Ett mer kast innan schaktföraren kommer hem.

Ett till

Ett till

Huset av den längsta natten

De var rovfåglar, formskiftade, sammanfogade,
svävande över vårdammen i den förlorade kanjonen,
sökandes efter den grotta de båda visste var där.

Vingarna vikta till sidan, de dök igenom portalmörker,
till botten, in i glödande ljus, fångade termik ovanför
ett stengolv och en ring av vita hästar.

En jord

ett hjärta,

trumslag,

samma slag,

läkning,

i huset av den

längsta natten.

Det var hög mark ovanför dammen och ingången till kanjonen. Skookum dök upp där strömmen gick in i dammen som en våravrinning.

Tillsammans gick de in i kanjonen. Skookum bad honom hitta en slät sten och blåsa in rädsla i den. De begravde stenen bland en stor talls rötter och satt vid det trädet en stund; han och Skookum, hans allierade.

Låt blå

renögon

bli till guld,

solstånd till solstånd,

vinter till sommar

Ut ur mörkret

in i ljuset.

Han bad Skookum att träffas vid vårdammen. När han
vandrade genom ängen för att hälsa Skookum tittade
han bakåt över sin axel.

De satt under tallen och ett ljus kom ner genom
grenarna, genom dem in i jorden. De log åt varandra
och Skookum frågade, "Varför tittar du tillbaka?"

Gångjärnet,

en pivå,

på svängande grind

eller dörr.

Fram och tillbaka,

minnen släpps

i passerandet av,

ett rum,

en äng,

till nästa.

Skookum ledde honom till det heliga trädet, klättrade med honom och knuffade honom bortom tallens räckvidd, in i den övre världen. När han anlände hälsades han av en sámi noaidi och bjöds in till en lávvu för att sitta vid elden.

Trumman dök upp, prydd med linjer och symboler ritade på lädret. Noaidi instruerade honom att utforma en karta av sina resor och dela den uråldriga kunskapen.

Lämna denna jordliga plats,

lås fast på en vektor,

förvänta dig inget slut.

Flyg över norrskenet,

dansa på horisonten.

Häng band,

tappa smulor,

märk träd—återvänd,

till avlägsna trummor.

Oulankas röster

Vi stannade i skogen,
vid floden, för kaffe.
Händer knäppta i knät,
han sade med tystad röst,
mummo kan se sjukdom och
kommande död. Hon var en boterska.
De sjuka togs till henne
istället för till en doktor.
Hon skylde sina krafter genom att använda
förband och skogsörter
när hon läkte,
för att inte bli kallad en häxa.

Jag kom för det här.
Fyller min själ med platser,
kaffeceremonier i skogen,
berättelser som började med mummo,
vetandes, seendes.
Gamla män stirrandes in i eld,
återkallar råd, varningar,
tar med allt till naturen för läkning.

Mummo sade, *"När du*
går till skogen med
pappa måste du vara tyst om
du vill se rävarna."

Och jag minns, *"Morfar,*
när vi går i skogen,
hör jag röster."

Skyfixers dagbok

Det är viskningstid.
Efter dagsljus,
innan soluppgång.
Du mediterar i tystnad,
lyssnar för luckor i
ljud och tanke.

Från den här sittplatsen, ovanför
Camp Creek Canyon, föreställer du dig
Chief Josephs hästar, kvinnor i filtar.
Dina ögon rör sig längs deras väg och du
inser att du inte är den första som gråter här.

Din trumma talar om
   bilder inuti bilder,
   resor inuti resor,
   metafor inuti metafor;
   masker av uråldriga hemligheter.

Höj din samejojk,
till andarna
 av prärien,
 av soluppgången,
 av guider och hjälpare,
 av jorden.

Vatten, titta vad du har
gjort. Välkomna droppandet.
Absorbera artefakter från
skiktade landskap,
konvergens av kronologi.

Alla svar är ännu inte tydliga.
Vissa funna i en portal,
i en kanjon,
precis ovanför horisonten.

När de sista ekona av
trumslag
rumlar till prärien,
försvagas dina knän,
andningen arbetar.

Den här resan är inte över.

Klargrönt ljud rör sig
genom ditt huvud;
musik hörd och sedd.

Inte skalor av din
barndom i A-moll;
ingen längtan i dessa
hopfulla ackord.

Sedan—fågelsång:

Västlig ängstrupial
Aftonsparv

Ute ur skuggorna

*En ceremoni hölls för en åldrande soldat. Efter fem
decennier belönades en veteran med en medalj, för skador
som hade drabbat hans själ.*

*Röster kunde höras från en avlägsen sjö i Sápmi. Unga
återfunna själsdelar,—tokiga, lekfulla och pratsamma—
kom för att deltaga i ceremonin. De var glada att vara
tillbaka. Det var mycket glädje och firande.*

*Soldaten eskorterades från paradmarkerna av en ensam
vit häst.*

När förlorar en soldat
delar av själen?
Vilket ögonblick markerar
den tysta bortgången?
När rädsla ökar?
Eller när rädsla förloras?
Fly, vänta,
göm dig bland djur och läkande andar,
överlev.

IX

Norwegian Translations

Translated to Norwegian by:

May Iren Hjorthaug, New Malden, U.K.

Deep River Finn	Deep River Finn
Onkalo	Onkalo
Dividing the Farm	Dele gården
You Took a Wrong Turn	Du gikk feil vei
Forester's Prayer	Skogvokterens bønn
Eulogy	Minneord
House of the Longest Night	Huset med den lengste natten
Voices of Oulanka	Stemmene i Oulanka
Skyfixer Journal	Himmelfikserens notisbok
Out of the Shadows	Ut av skyggene

Deep River Finn

Natur er ensomhet,
ikke ment som underholdning.
Bli hjemme, min venn,

la meg stille min lengsel.

Ved soloppgang
i Willapa Hills,
begynner rødstrupen,
solo, a cappella.

Onkalo

Finsk for gjemmested

Vend tilbake til et sted
du en gang bodde,
finn noe
du en gang mistet.

Hold på uskadde
deler av sjel og selv
mens dugg legger seg
i lavlandet.

Finn sedertrestubben
brent hul,
lukk døren ved
sverdbregnen,
let etter barnlige gjenstander
gravd ned der.

Ta på flate steiner
fra flyktig vann,
si *himmelfikser*,
si *drømmestrøm*.

Gråt,
gråt endelig,
for gutten.

Dele gården

Du tar gjerder,
dyrkede marker,
rette linjer,
skarpe hjørner,
hvert dekar.
Gi meg
svingende
elveløp, bredde med
dunkjevle, piletre.

Du tar skogsbruk,
klart avgrenset.
Gi meg
gjengrodd sump,
kolle over myr hvor
salt møter ferskt,
vårdam hvor
salamandere kommer
en vårnatt fra
trerester under bakken.

Du gikk feil vei

ved sukkerbusken,
dens rustne sevjebøtter og kobberkjele
spredt utover skogbunnen.

Hvis du hadde vasset langs elven Katy
og gått oppover den gamle grusveien,
ville du ha kommet til
holtet med sølvlind, lønn
og gulbjørk.

Du kunne ha funnet det
hemmelige rommet i sandsteingrotten
med bregner på veggene
og blader på gulvet.

I stedet tok du veien til
buen av beverdammen,
rundt vårdammen og
inn i den glemte canyonen.

Jeg lurte på om du hørte
svartstrupenattergalen, svartbrystparulaen
eller eremittskogtrosten på den
tette, fuktige, frodige vannbunnen.

Jeg lurte på om du fant et sted
hvor asken kunne begynne sin reise
nedetter de våryre bekkene,
til elven Deer, gjennom Superior, til sjøen.

Skogvokterens bønn

Trærne er min katedral,
våryre bekker min dåp,
snøtruger min livbøye.

Stillhet min meditasjon,
blåskriken min vokter,
spirende lønnetrær lovnaden.

Åndeguiden, mitt kompass,
hjelper meg å gå dit jeg burde gå,
gjøre det jeg burde gjøre.

Minneord

Til Marie, den beste fordømte fiskerkvinnen en
bulldosersjåfør
kunne håpet å ha kjent.

Det var de siste av de beste dagene.

Dieselrøyk og mineraljord,
den gode marka lukter av hogst
i øvre Naselle.

Ned strømmen,
den ujevne bakken ved elvebredden
tok imot den nyfangede regnbueørreten,
fra munnen hang en okie-drifter.

Ett kast til før doserkjøreren kommer hjem.

Ett til

Ett til

Huset med den lengste natten

De var rovfugler, hamløpere, forent, i svev over
vårdammen i dalen i den glemte canyonen, på leting
etter hulen de begge visste var der.

Med vinger foldet til siden, stupte de gjennom portalens
mørke, til bunnen, inn i glødende lys, fanget en termikk
over et steingulv og en sirkel av hvite hester.

En jord

ett hjerte,

trommerytme,

samme rytme,

helbredelse,

i huset med

den lengste natten.

Der var en forhøyning over dammen og inngangen til canyonen. Skookum kom til syne der elven rant inn i dammen som smeltevann.

Sammen gikk de inn i canyonen. Skookum ba ham finne en glatt stein og blåse frykt inn i den. De begravde steinen blant røttene til en stor furu og satt ved treet en stund; han og Skookum, hans allierte.

La blå

reinsdyrøyne

bli til gull,

solverv til solverv,

vinter til sommer.

Ut av mørket

inn i lys.

Han ba Skookum om å møtes ved vårdammen. Da han gikk gjennom enga for å treffe Skookum, så han seg tilbake over skulderen.

De satt under furua og et lys kom ned gjennom greinene, gjennom dem, inn i jorda. De smilte mot hverandre og Skookum spurte: "Hvorfor ser du deg tilbake?"

Hengslet,

et dreiepunkt,

på svingende port

eller dør.

Frem og tilbake,

minner forløses

flyktig,

ett rom,

en eng,

til det neste.

Skookum tok ham til det hellige treet, klatret med ham og dyttet ham forbi rekkevidden til furua, til den øvre verden. Da han kom frem ble han møtt av en samisk noaide, og invitert inn i en lavvo for å sitte ved bålet.

Trommen kom ut, pyntet med tegninger av linjer og symboler på skinnet. Noaiden ba ham lage et kart over sine reiser og dele den gamle visdommen.

Forlat dette jordiske stedet,

lås på en vektor,

ikke forvent en slutt.

Fly over nordlyset,

dans i horisonten.

Heng opp bånd,

strø smuler,

brenn trær—vend tilbake,

ved lyden av fjerne trommerytmer.

Stemmene i Oulanka

Vi stanset i skogen,
ved elven, for en kopp kaffe.
Med hendene foldet i fanget,
sa han lavmælt:
mummo kunne se sykdom og
forestående død. Hun var en healer.
De syke ble ledet til henne
i stedet for en lege.
Hun skjulte kreftene sine ved å bruke en
tourniquet og skogsurter
når hun helet,
for ikke å bli kalt en heks.

Jeg kom for dette.
For å fylle sjelen min med steder,
kaffeseremonier i skogen,
historier som begynte med mummo,
som visste, som så.
Gamle menn stirrer inn i ilden,
minnes råd, advarsler,
tar alle til naturen for helbredelse.

Mummo sa: *"Når du
drar til skogen med
pappa må du være stille hvis du
vil se revene."*

Og jeg husker: *"Bestefar,
når vi går i skogen,
hører jeg stemmer."*

Himmelfikserens notisbok

Det er hvisketid.
Etter dagslys,
før soloppgang.
Du mediterer i stillhet,
lytter etter pauser mellom
lyd og tanke.

Fra denne plassen, ovenfor
Camp Creek Canyon, tenker du på
Chief Josephs hester, kvinner med tepper.
Øynene dine beveger seg langs ruten deres og du
innser at du ikke er den første som gråter her.

Trommen din snakker om
    bilder inne i bilder,
    reiser inne i reiser,
    metafor inne i metafor;
    masker av gamle hemmeligheter.

Ta din samiske joik,
til åndene
   av prærien,
   av soloppgangen,
   av veiledere og hjelpere,
   av jorden.

Vann, se hva du har
gjort. Ta imot kildevellet.
Merk deg detaljene
i lagdelte landskaper,
det kronologiske sammenfallet.

Ikke alle svarene er tydelige ennå.
Noen er funnet i en portal,
i en canyon,
like over horisonten.

Idet de siste ekkoene fra
trommerytmer
buldrer ut mot prærien,
vekner knærne dine,
pusten river.

Denne reisen er ikke over.

Lysgrønn lyd strømmer
gjennom hodet ditt;
musikk hørt og sett.

Ikke skalaer
i a-moll fra din barndom;
ingen lengsel i disse
håpefulle klangene.

Deretter—fuglesang:

    Prærielerketrupial

    Vesperspurv

Ut av skyggene

Det ble holdt en seremoni for en aldrende soldat. Etter femti år ble en krigsveteran tildelt en medalje for sjelesmerten han pådro seg.

Stemmer kunne høres fra en fjern sjø i Sápmi. Unge gjenfunnede deler av sjelen—tøysete, lekne, og pratsomme—kom og deltok i seremonien. De var glade for å være tilbake. Det var en feiring fylt av glede.

Soldaten ble eskortert fra paradeområdet av en enslig hvit hest.

Når mister en soldat
deler av sin sjel?
Hvilket øyeblikk markerer
den stille bortgangen?
Følelsen av frykt?
Eller når frykten er borte?
Flykt, vent,
gjem deg blant dyr og helbredende ånder,
overlev.

Acknowledgements

Gratitude to Dr. John Reynolds, PhD, Psychologist. In my estimation a healer, a shaman. If truth be known, he saved my life. I found him by accident, but I do not believe in accidents.

All respect and honor to the Suquamish Warriors Veterans Center for guiding me and other veterans in the difficult process of obtaining benefits for the wounds of war.

W. S. Merwin, "The River of Bees," from *The Second Four Books of Poems* (Port Townsend, Washington: Copper Canyon Press, 1993). Copyright © 1993 W. S. Merwin.

Nils-Aslak Valkeapää, *BEAIVI, ÁHČÁŽAN*, DAT O.S., N-9520, Guovdageaidnu, Norway, 1988

The poems in Chapter I previously appeared in *Bunchgrass and Buttercups*, 2012, and *My Finnish Soul*, 2010, both published by Shelter Bay Publishing, Bainbridge Island, Washington. Copyright © Gary

V Anderson. These poems were also included in a limited copy production for a Nature Conservancy Poetry in Place event at Onota Camp in the Upper Peninsula of Michigan, September 18, 2017.

Three poems were selected by ARS Poetica in Bremerton, Washington, and inspired artistic works. "All About Bracken"/*I am the boy under bracken*, by Dawn Jarvela Henthorn, "You Took a Wrong Turn," by Steve Parmelee and "Dividing the Farm"/*Dichotomy,* by Susan Blackburn.

The poems, "The House of the Longest Night," "Out of the Shadows" and "Skyfixer Journal" appeared in other forms with other titles in *Outpost 2015, Writings from the Zumwalt Prairie,* Fishtrap Outpost and *Everyday It Happens,* 2017, Fishtrap Outpost.

A portion of the poem, "Voices of Oulanka," appeared in an article published by MTV Finland (MTV.fi), September 23, 2018, answering the question, "Why is Gary in Finland?" Marjanna Wikman, producer.

The author appeared on a segment (part 4) of a documentary film produced by SVT, Swedish Public Television, *Från Sápmi till Alaska,* to discuss views expressed in the first paragraph of the Introduction to this book of poetry. SVT was in Poulsbo, Washington following in the footsteps of Sámi reindeer herders sent from Sápmi to Alaska in 1894, to teach reindeer herding to indigenous Alaskans. Some of the descendants migrated to Poulsbo in the early 1900's. Sophia Nordin, Producer, August Sandstrom, Videographer, Maret Steinfjell, Reporter.

Thank you so much to the translators: Ritva Torikka, Northern Sámi, Sonia Luokkala, Finnish, Linnea Lindblom, Swedish, and May Iren Hjorthaug, Norwegian.

SKYFIXER was expertly designed, typeset and edited by Ashley Muehlbauer.

Thanks for all the understanding and love from my family, Roberta, Justin, Suvarna, Tyler, Arik and Deven.

GARY V ANDERSON identifies as a Finnish American poet, though he is also Swede and Norwegian—and has Sámi ancestors. He was raised on forty acres in Deep River, Washington. His dad was a logger and his mother never learned to drive. Gary remembers hearing the last whistle of the last steam train to empty logs in Deep River. He dropped out of college only to be scooped up as fodder for the Vietnam war and was forty before he attained adulthood. His new goal is to become an elder before he becomes an ancestor.

Gary has been moderator for spoken word events at Finnish-American Folk Festivals in Naselle, Washington and Finn Fest USA events in Astoria, Oregon and Hancock, Michigan. He has been a frequent featured poet at the Poulsbohemian in Poulsbo, Washington, Free Range Poetry in Portland, Oregon and on Lyle Haataja's Scandinavian Hour radio show in Astoria, Oregon.

Gary and his wife spent nearly ten years in the Upper Peninsula of Michigan, in Shelter Bay, on Deer Lake.

They lived at the end of the road, twenty miles from the grocery store, removed from ambient light, and recall walking out on the frozen lake in snowshoes to see the comet Hale-Bop in one quadrant of the sky and a partial eclipse of the moon in another.

While in Michigan, Gary was involved in the Northern Great Lakes Forest Project, a conservation easement on 271,000 acres of timberland that connected more than 2 million acres of wilderness in the Upper Peninsula. The project protected more than 660 lakes, 500 miles of rivers and streams and 52,000 acres of wetlands.

Gary and Roberta also granted a conservation easement on 244 acres of land at the west end of Deer Lake, now owned by The Nature Conservancy.

The journey back to his true self began in these wild places. They are an integral part of him, and though he is rarely there in person, he visits often.

Skookum 16, 18
Viet Nam PTSD theapy 24
(Karl Marlantes)
"memories released" p 19
Onkalo p. 6

Made in the USA
Columbia, SC
16 September 2020

19879824R00098